AUTHENTIC THOUGHTS

Basvi Reddy

QUICK READS

by Writersgram Publications

AUTHENTIC THOUGHTS

Poetry by Basvi Reddy

First Impression: February 2020

ISBN: 978-9389244496

Published by: Writersgram Publications, New Delhi
Imprint: Quick Reads

www.writersgram.com
publications@writersgram.com

Inspired By

Purnanadh Rachapudi

When I sound your breath
It tugs me unintentionally
Towards you

#You

Every time you fail,
You discover a new caliber of yours,
So be valiant to see the real new you

#New You –Find Yourself

Beauty is where you look at a person,
But not with any filtered……
Artificial alterations…

#Simple Me

Believe in your aspire, strive it
The wind of triumph with love turns to you,
Don't be desperate,
A rosy glorious dawn is waiting for you

#Believe In Self

Love the life you got,

Live your passion,dream…

Laugh every moment of life…

Limit yourself according to the context

&

At the end of the day it's all about you,

To be happy

#Try To Be Happy

Notion of your s seek my attention,

Your wary, make me insane…

Yours everything, make me go crazy……

#You

Strong women won't beg,

Instead she grabs everything,

&

Fix them herself

#Self Strong Woman

You never know the value of your stone…
Unless and until you shape it in to a gem

#Be Out Of Comfort Zone

You stand first for nation …… far from your ones,
You make us sleep with a hope to have a beautiful morning,
We can't repay the debt of your hecatomb…

#A Bow To Army Men

Never chase people who, doesn't belong to you…
Rather focus in yourself
Never degrade yourself being after people,
Never beg to things to done by others,
Never ruin beautiful present,
Never care people, who aren't for you,
Rather fall in love with your confused, noisy, naked soul

#Slef Love

Every soul is beautiful the way you look it,
So, adopt new ways to deal with naked souls

#Every Beautiful Soul

When I sound of every regal field,

Make me exhilarate to see you…

&

Every drive has driven me close to you, since first drive……

#You

Ignorance of you keep me wait for you

I don't know to make a step towards you……

Instead loving you from distance

#You

Go beyond limits to know

What immense beauty is all about……

#Beauty Is All Around

Every time I try to raise up with expectations to touch
sky, People never let me try at least,
You can limit me but cannot limit up my independent soul,
Where my soul, never give up a hope to touch the sky of my
dreams………

#Keep Self Motivating

Despite of many despair things around me,
A spark of hope remain me to wait for you,
Nevertheless, I would never see you again,
But I want you to be mine

#You

A strong women can choose her
Priority without any male concern

#Strong Women

Ultimate destiny is one night taking a long breath,
Feel happy & counting starts in infinity universe

#Relaxed

People say I am divers when it comes to relationships…..
Actually my priority isn't a relationship

 # I Am –Me

It has to happen to you,
Like how it happened to me,
And
When you meet a right one,
Am sure you will cross all norms which you made to self……
Like I crossed mine norms……

#In Wait For You

Choices we make today, is our destiny
So be wise enough to choose from your possibility

#Be Conscious

In chasing success,
Everyone established grappling with each other,
And skipped to be happier,
Then started investing in how to be happy…
But literally being blissful is within you,
So begin to rediscover the real you…….

#Be Happy

Don't limit yourself to the norms made by society ……
In reality society is ignorant of your happiness
Open door to,
Let the storm of happiness hit you

#Cross Rules

Strangers we meet………
Some of them get connected,
Some of those are friends,
Friends whom, we get closer,
We laugh, advise, confront, love, each other
At some day we sustain for each other,
Best comfort zone after family………

#Love My Besties

#Bestie Love

Love without esteem and gratitude,
Doesn't blossom a relationship

#Respect Each Relationsheep

She is battling with in,

At least to put out the choices she made…….

She is battling with in,

At least to put out the aspirations she dreamt

She is battling between her ones and her desire,

And one day her anxious inner voice may hit like a storm ……

And that stroke of storm is uncatchable

But she won't make any compromise……

 # My Voice

I attempt and I try……

But I don't, loose hope and I never give up,

I plan, and I plot ……

And if you say me a bitch am okay with it……

Because it's my part of play not yours

#Stay Strong

Never ever judge someone,

Just observe their intentions and reply with your action

#No Judgement

Hey open up yourself,

Fall in love with your zesty self,

Go beyond limits to feel yourself

#Feel The Real You

Best part of life is meeting you

&

Falling for you,

Let the life last for a second

Let that second be yours,

&

Falling for you reveals a new shade of mine to me…..

#You

We go through variant context of life,

We meet few who love us, likes us, hurts us, leave us,

But it's quite unique to encounter & stay with one who hates us ……

Anyways ignore who are jealous on us

 # Ignore Things

Scared of being failure, loosing you,

Scared of putting my word around,

Fear of losing everything ….

Rather,

I want to love me, flew as far as I can

I want to be happy, as happier I could …

&

Never care for one,

And if fate changes I wish I could see u as mine

#Scary Of Losing

Never put yourself respect a side,

In chase of others,

Don't, loose attitude in race of holding others……

Don't be anxious, stressed……

One day will certainly be all yours, wait patiently

#Be Patient

Between unknowing and annoying people,
A beautiful soul found,
Showered lots of love,
Brought my smile back
&
Showed how sly people are

#Be Aware Of Good People

We make choices,
Life shows us possibilities,
And we make modifications,
Though we may flunk or get success
But we satisfy with efforts on attempts we made
And one day success knocks us

 # Keep On Motivating

You can't descend confidence and
Focus towards your passion
You can't stop loving yourself and your credibility
Unless and until you accomplish yourself

#Love Yourself For Wt U Are

Most powerful weapon to ruin is woman beauty

And

A greedy man's thirsty would ruin him,

By chasing a beauty

 # No Greedy

Don't dream to be someone's queen someday

Rather be a self-made woman,

Go get everything u wish and create your class

#Selfmade Woman

Yup, I don't like when another girl is on your bike……

Yes, your ignorance pulls me to you

And yes the way you breath

It attracts me and your elegance id my obsession

#YOU

Fill yourself by

Accomplishing yourself

#Self Love

Love passionately happens…

And won't calculate the ranges

It just happens

#Love

I don't know how passionately I began to like you……

I don't know how I became this mad about you…….

But I just love you

And I wish this fate would bring us together

#Littel Of Love And Hope

Deity of our existence is

Mother earth

Queen of generous is

Mother earth

Divinity of tolerance is

Mother earth

Majesty of beauty is

Mother earth

And holds us with no expectations

In her lap after out death,

And I bow my head to you

Mother earth

#No Planet 2

Karma is reflection of
Your own choice and actions
Be conscious to choose your karma

 # Be Careful To Choose

Don't scrutinize past contexts,
It will ruin present and peace of mind

#Leave Past

If you won't let the things go,
It won't let you go further

#Bye Bye Past

We meet as strangers but destined to be together

And togetherness of us is limitless,

Protect ourselves by beyond limiting,

Last bench ties us together………

Emptiness is when you are absent

After long arguments, we still have fun,

You are phenomenal in my life

My dearest bestie

I love you and us

#Last Benchers

#Friendhsip Goals

Darken sky has twinkling stars

As well,

Darken aspects gives zeal to twinkle

#Zeal To Be The One

Clangs are inaudible

When inner voice bursts with in

#Inner Voice

May be food is just a tiny meal for,

Who waste it….

Remind yourself

So many are struggling out for a tiny bite of nosh

#No Food Wastage

Though we are longer in distance from years,

Such tiny talks put us together

Much love between us shows long distance relationships works

Mine and your friendship goals last forever

#Friendship Goals

When you pee on her lap she

Enjoys her motherhood

In elderliness you offer them old age homes……

Truth is you are abandoning your humanity

#Mom

No matter how hollow life throws you in darkness

where, their isn't ray of light

But it's you to stand by yourself in search of ray of light

#Thirsty Of Success

People with hope,
Will never quit

#Don't Quit

Scale of success isn't measured by increasing of asset,
It is measured by one's version and vision

#Diffrent Vision On Success

My happiness is not in what you gifted me,
It's in within me,
And one day you will know,
It was never part of mine…
And that day you will regret for what,
You gifted me….

#Never Decide For Others

Relationships should be triggers healthily
But shouldn't be comportment

#Relationships

Protect your child as much as u can,
But don't protect as such as
They might suffer from suffocation

#Suffocation

How tightly you hold relationships
They become that fragile and rigid to fix

#Don't Hold Anyone

I hated things, till I met you
I wanted to stop it, but I couldn't
I thoughts is wasn't normal, but it was phenomenal with all,
I was gracefully tugged by your soul,
As it is you, am waiting with tearful of hope

#You In Dream

Farming isn't a profession it is a way of life
Educate your child to farm and plant……
Its best way of life

#No Cheap Look For Farming

AS much as you pull me down to down,
I will, raise as far as such you couldn't catch me
As much as tight you hold me,
I will free as such as you couldn't find me
As long as you try to clutch me,
For sure you will lose everything from my side

#Self Respect

#Keep Believe In Self

You may suppress my capabilities,
But not my thoughts to catch myself……

#Be Independent

#Love To Live In My Choice

Limiting and spacing between each other
Blossom a blissful relationship

#Happy Relationships

I wish this wind around me would communicate you,
And say how prior you are to me
I wish this wind around me would communicate you,
And say how vigorously I need you
I wish this wind around me would communicate you,
And tell how authentic I am
I wish this wind around me would tell you
How passionate I am about you

#Dream
#You

I am not someone's spare time
I fill my time by being my self

#Self Love

Every aspect of life you are with me,
Never let me scare of anything,
Carried all my anger and stupidity
Never stopped to love me and how could I forget,
You care of my, such tiny things
You always been my second parent and my life line

#Best Brother Ever
 # I Love You

It is that I am comfort with,
What you are
It is that everyone search of perfection
But I found you……..
Your every piece of thing, make me comfort
I wish I could be,
Your zone of comfort and confidence

#Us

 # Comfort Zone

#No One Is Perfect-

Writing makes me fall in love
More with myself

#Do What You Love

Little little adjustments make wonders
And apparent tiny changes ties us together
And gives little more of happy memories

#Adjustments Blossoms Relationships

Random thoughts of you,

Brings me a wider smile

When I dream about us

I wish us to be together

Which it seems to be,

but

Might not happen anymore,

I wish I had lived in dream

#Hope

#You

Don't regret for mistakes happened unknowingly

Instead try to fix or resolve them

#Try

Why am unable to say ‘no’
To what I don’t like
Why am unable to say ‘no’
To what I don’t want
Why am unable to say ‘no’
And move on……….
Unable to say no is my biggest error
I should learn to say ‘no’
I guess, I could able to do it

 # Say No

How good you might be or a bad person
There is a back talk behind you

#Back Talks

I thought life would be easier if I won’t fall for anyone
But It was fate to fall for you and
I began to like you, know you
At last
I hope things would have worked for me too

#Seek Of Little Hope

I want to say louder and louder
That I am free from all mess,
I prepared to accept everything
And
I will do everything I wished to do………
I believe in me

#Believe In Me

Wind is polluted
Yup we did it
Tress are dying
Yup we did it
Animal species are vanishing
We are foremost to let them end
As far as I know we, humans are kindest species ever
But where is this kindness gone?
I don't know
WHAT MESSAGE ARE WE GIVING TO FUTURE GENERATIONS
Destruction, or to spread humanity

#No Planet 2 # Save Earth

#Save Yourself

From a drastic catastrophe trauma
We would get something to learn from it or
To decide what to do from it

 # Learn From What Happened And Do

As long as you let the fire lit in
Yourself and flow grimly,
It will take you
Where you belong to

#Go On Flow And Glow

Leader must be a root of plant
But not a blessed flower,
Which is at top and show off

#Leader Ship Quality

Not only increasing influence in people but a leader,

Should be a need to his people

Not only to lead people but a leader,

Should stand with his people

Not only ensuring people but also,

Should keep uttered words……

But not the one who ensures before elections

 # Not Only A Promising Leader

Relationships are related to us,

Until we relate us to them

But once we give up,

There is no longer a ship between to two river banks……

 # Be Careful To Hold Relations

You are with me every time,
Whenever I needed you
You carried all,
My bunch of emotions
Your love made me,
Stronger and stronger
You held, me with
Every inch of love you could do to me
You been a second mom to me
I wish everyone would have a,
Beastie like you………… like I have you

#To My Cloesest Bestie

I thought to love you
As long it is possible
Then I question to self
Is loving a person can end?
Yeah, later I knew loving is giving your self
Every inch that you can do

#Respect Your Love

#Donot Count, What You Do For

If you take advantage of my silence
Then you will be responsible for my roar

#Do Don't Understimate

After a failure love story,
It's always seen a boy addicted to alcohol
But it is not seen,
A sorrow face behind a girls fake smile face

#Love Is Love To All

I don't need,
A king to fill my kingdom
I can form
A, Queendom to by myself

#Queendom

#Be Strong

Never regret on sacrifices,
What you do to your own
Because things are being sacrificed to lead a betterment and
Do sacrifices things with fulfillment

#Sacrifice For Happy Life

Why man is respected based on,
Measurement of success
But not by beauty of his soul

#Soul Beauty

Don't fall for a boy who impresses you
Fall for a man, who inspires you,
Because he teaches, your worth and to love yourself…

#Manhood

Days are passing, seasons are changing
But my obsession on you, didn't change
While, I thank the universe and divine nature for creation of you
And, I thank the wind which flown between us and brought us together
But it is only you,
I miss hardly

#You

We don't need a leader who stands for us
We need a leader who stands with us
And
One who is with us, are among us only

#Leader Is Among You

When things aren't possible ......
I started to look for you in others
Again I realize it is you
Which I can't find in anyone else

#You, Specally You

Being a creature in this unending universe,
Why variations in range and status
Being a human after all,
Why judgments among us
I wish one day, there must be no state of status

#Human Is Human

#All Are Equal

Though the entire universe don't believe in you,
It is only you, to stand by yourself
Thought this entire world don't understand you,
It is only you, to build your strength
Thought the world around you, don't believe in you
It is that you need not prove your worth
Because success at someone's point of view
Doesn't prove your worth
And one cannot decide your success

#Keep Believe In You

May be you are millionaire or billionaire
You cannot eat mental of currency you earned
You only eat is food
So be kind to those who are in need of food

#Respect Food

Anger is emotion and is human instinct
While in anger control your tone
Because emotion is controlled and not instinct

#Anger Is Dangerous

If there is no extreme intensity of
Madness and Insanity
Then it is no longer called
LOVE

#Love

Don't shrink where you don't belong to
You are already far grown up and
You know where to set up
Yourself

#Be Yourself

Applying your inner voice,
May not always give a positive result
Or
It may turn out a drastic mistake
But
I could feel pleasured because it was me,
Who chosen to make it

#Applying Yourslef Gives Inner Peace

As we apply others voice
Then we always belong to others,
Not us by self

#Love What Your Inner Voice Speake

Whatever you choose,
At some point you give in everything to it.
And giving yourself in to it,
Is what you loved
And you call it hard work
But I call it "love"
"MY LOVE IS WHAT I DO"

#Love What You Do

Don't let anyone search your imperfections,
Instead find them by self
Because if others point out,
Your soul will go low or fire will lit inside you
But if you find by yourself you will
Love and accept them

#Self Love

Suna tha ae dil hai mushkil

Patha natha ithna mushkil ki

Bus may dewani hogayi

Bus tera ek nazar se

#Deewangi

One says am unlucky

One says am in bad phase

And good phase

But I call it as part of life which, all need to go through

#Be Positive

ALL will enjoy and see only fruits, flowers

But no one notices the root of plant which is strong

From plant grown to tree

#Dont Only See, Success

www.ingramcontent.com/pod-product-compliance
Ingram Content Group UK Ltd.
Pitfield, Milton Keynes, MK11 3LW, UK
UKHW040038200726
13845UKWH00054B/467

9 789389 244496